A River
PENETRATING THE
Soul Line

BOOK #II

KEVIN HAMLETT

ISBN 978-1-969865-36-7 (Paperback)
ISBN 978-1-969865-37-4 (Ebook)

Inquiries and Book Orders should be addressed to:

Leavitt Peak Press
17901 Pioneer Blvd Ste L #298, Artesia, California 90701
Phone #: 2092191548

A River Penetrating the Soul

A River of Words has the growing capacity to mend, mold, and memorialize us into a compact vessel, flowing into an English Channel while the waters churn and shuffle, leaving behind a powerful ripple effect.

Contents

Dare to Dream

Part II

Dare to Dream beyond the bloody and murky path of death and doubt;
Yet spring ahead until thick clusters of Sunflowers soon sprout about;
Dare to Dream beyond the cold, clamorous shout of the musty Greyhound that pouts;
Move ahead unflinchingly toward that fresh and glittering route;
Dare to Dream beyond the bitter course of the Unrestored—unarticulated, surprisingly tempest-tossed drearily into an entangled sphere of dangling dross now sinking down steadily into the sullen ground; once unearthed—all-round pearls that were once bound rubies in *Jail Town;*
Somehow I must also resist the monumental tides of shaded stereotypes and paled prejudices with relentless rigor, vigor, and rhythm yet remaining *unflowered;*

Once more I must affirm that I will not be easily
Moved....................
Defeated.................
Worn.....................
Scathed..................
Or
Even Screwed..............
Unsheathed from the Scabbard—THE WORD that, though it pierces me before the Divine, yet unquestionably heals me, unto which the once perpetually downtrodden is now transformed into an unparalleled creature that is divinely newfound;

That is unquestionably an inimitable Indian pipe set preciously upon the Unmovable Mound;
That is unthinkably found as beautiful ducklings floating gently upon the plus riverbanks of the Jordan Surround;
So I must think beyond the puny drapes that sizzle upon the Blistered. Barren Lands of Complacency:
So I must think beyond the dry-rotted walls of fear that try to enclose, nagging at my every fantasy:
So I must think beyond the DUSK WORDS—"dum-dum, block-head, or dunbred"—uttered unequivocally, meant to subdue me;
So I must think beyond the conspiring termites of self-abnegation that try to summon the horrible words of death upon me.
And thereby move ahead triumphantly.
Though the dynamic words: "Dare to Dream" sometimes sound hackneyed to me as a google-eyed gorilla chewing the gross contents of a spoiled, rotten banana.
Though these magnificent words sometimes sound as trite as my own cooing and wagging, a chew-chew panting for a bristled bone found along the trail inside a narrow, tall gate of China.
Though these powerful words sometimes sound as trite as a maiden viewing her full field of corn, carrot, and cotton, yet in a world, however, that is overarching with fierce criticism, malice, and animosity, the POTENT WORDS—"Dare to Dream"—become irreplaceable, like ox horns in the reservoir of my mind, ready to scratch indelibly across the cerebral pages of my heart and mind, those fresh and fulfilling words.
So here again, I affirm that I must Dare to Dream of a better world gladly emerging into sight:
Dare to Dream that I'll soar insurmountably beyond the dismal night;
Dare to Dream that I'll surmount vigorously over any plight;
While sometimes shaken, yet not overtaken;
While sometimes discouraged, yet not depressed;
While sometimes fearful, yet not perturbed;
Hence, dare to imagine a better day that is well beyond the ominous clouds of calamity.

And yet still see vividly splendid cream caps spring marvelously from life's barren soils.
And yet still see widely brilliant inky seas spring marvelously from life's deserted soils.
And yet still see widely brilliant high hawk soaring wonderfully beyond the flat marshlands;
For every precious loss, there is inevitable gain;
For a radiant hope, henceforth, remains.
Oh yes!
Dare to Dream.
Dare to Dream.
Dare to Dream.
Beyond the psychological woes that contribute to a grim and painful past.
Beyond the thick huge cloudbanks of obscurity, thereby blocking the glittering and gorgeous course beyond the Scottish Terrier that howls and growls for miles.
Oh yes! Far beyond every conceivable barrier.
For a clear vision can penetrate beyond the thick walls of a now burst bubble and thus touches poignantly the minds and hearts of everyone who embraces it.
If my passion to envision does not go beyond the narrow confines of the humdrums or the routines, then my dream will fade gradually like soap suds sinking inside the huge hot tub of hopelessness.
So I must Dare to Dream if no other mortal will take on the challenge of embracing that remarkable and blazing torch of envisioning for a better day and way, thus hoping beyond this decade and far beyond any foul fossils of decay.

Aphorisms

A Reputable Name
A reputable name is like a good crop sown in the earth; it continues to produce fruit and thereby replenishes the land.

Better Days Ahead
Beyond the thick clad soot, there is a fresh fountainhead ahead.

Great Awakenings
Sometimes it takes an enormous earthquake to awaken the human species from slumber and sloth.

Not Quitting
When you are at a brink of a breakthrough, do not succumb to quitting, for it is precisely then that you will indeed move on, thereby seeing the splendid rainbow surrounding the clouds and sun.

Cultivation
Just as there is a need for both sun and rain to cultivate the earth continually, so too is there a need to have sun and rain to keep the heart cultivated continually.

On Knowledge
Knowledge is not power, but applied knowledge is power; one could have encyclopedic knowledge and yet not apply it, while one may have a paucity of knowledge and apply it with their whole heart.

Group Consensus

Adding Group Consensus to a sentence is not always complete and sweet; sometimes it is better to stand alone, with a firm peace of mind, than to follow blindly a mixed multitude, accompanied by disheartening pain, prolonged hardships and timeless disappointments brought about by fluctuating majority ties.

Apology

It does not diminish one's moral stature to apologize for a misunderstanding brought about by one toward another; in fact, an appropriate apology can only furnish one's heart and also heal any other jagged lumps attached to one's humanity.

Pleasing Others

To reach success by trying to please everyone can ultimately lead to displeasure, disappointment, loss of identity, and a loss of purpose in life, where ultimately no one is pleased.

Commitment

A heaven-bound commitment yields innumerable dividends—here and in the world to come.

Full Potential

A mortal cannot begin to reach his or her full potential without the wholehearted and painstaking efforts exacted of him or her.

Comforts of Complacency

It's easy to sip tea and lavish oneself under the comforts of complacency with accumulated wealth and an exuberant home.

The Heart of the Problem

The gruesome sight of rockets, bombs, or of ballistic missiles in the form of projected squids soaring against the grim and groaning sky, in a sense, stems from mankind's morbid internal explosiveness—the problematic source of the heart. So the WWI, WWII, and yes, what will even become perhaps the WWIII syndrome, may well be a prolonged commotion of internal strife between mankind, thereby triggering internal explosions that manifest as external combustions within even the ominous clouds of nuclear disaster that seek to obliterate mankind, erase a vision for a more peaceful world, and thereby create an unforgettable faux pas.

Victory

A victory easily won may be a victory not easily kept.

Life

Life, with its multiplicity of outcomes, can thrust one to pause—in meditation—for a healthy breviary along a brilliant path to tread, or to lag pensively along a shadowy path to tinker.

Honesty with Self

The great challenge, sometimes, is to face squarely those distorted aspects of the self and thereby admit that this is "no other than the down-and-out me" who desires a supernatural change for the better.

Calm after the Storm

After the intense turbulent storms rage within the celestial cage, there is an assured, remarkable calm recorded within the columns of His crested cosmic page.

Worthful Sacrifice

What's worth the sacrifice and the commitment is worth the life and the awaited outcome. Keep toiling in the soil; don't become spoiled or twisted in the coil. Stay renewed, steadfast, and hopeful. Your special day will come with a glowing cloudbank, resulting in what will become a radiant production: once in an obscure vacuumed path to trod, but now striding along the glittering path set in sod.

Life's Outcome Met with Hope

In life, there are undoubtedly moments of drought, this is no better time than to discover and store up that which replenishes and lasts. In life, there are undoubtedly moments of saturation, this is no better time than to demonstrate a developed poise in facing life's fertility, but all the more have an indomitable determination to remain creatively discontented hence reaching for new boundaries in life. Keep the wheel spinning and those special cogs in motion and your machine will turn toward a new and even stronger route or thrust. In reality life is about progressive growth and dynamic change. When the strong winds of tribulation come, their brutal aftermath can bring forth the best in humanity, fashioning oneself into an incandescent lamp from an age-old churn while the emerging glow remains remarkably timeless through this special and sacred medium. So the words "thriving hope" remains strikingly lit, arrayed, and thereby sealed within their precious yet durable medium.

Sword

I wield the sword that will carve for me the special straightway from the meandering path…I wield the sword that will separate me from the pale past, thus enabling me to live in the peaceful present and thereby allowing me to hope for the best in the forethought future…I wield the sword that will cut asunder any large deposits of doubts, fears, and mishaps. Oh yes torn to shreds are the badgering boulders of dangling dangers, droopy discouragements, and disappointing dooms.

Human Efficiency and Dynamics

An efficient, dynamic, and giant machine—with every cog, gear, and motor—works together in operation, functioning collectively yet performing each duty separately. There's neither clutter nor cutoff. So is this machine, in a sense, the analogy for human efficiency and human dynamics.

Divine Companionship

There is something special within every human being's sinews or tendons, wherein the desire—whether one knows it or not—is that significant symbiotic connection in the form of divine companionship.

Life: Long-Issues Neglected

Time after time the very issue of my heart that I have neglected reappears before me as a giant dagger, haunting both my present and my presence.

Mankind's Challenge
One of the great challenges for mankind is to face the "how longs?" of life.

A Highway—Salvation
At the byway, there is a highway; on the sideway, there is a highway; on the front way, there is a highway; at the midway, there is a highway; on the back way, there is a high way; on the runway, there is a highway; wherever you go, there is a highway of salvation and hope!

Injurious Thoughts
Shall I cast myself into the far-flung, pale ditch of pessimism through injurious thoughts?

A Diamond yet More
On the surface there is a Divinely endowed naturally fine beauty in all of us, but beneath that intangible surpleness lies a divinely crafted spirit that each of us can have, whereby there is an overarching design—each connecting and growing out of another—in reciprocal charity, grace, patience, and long-suffering. There is such a resplendence that can radiate in us far beyond the gushing glitter of an inanimate diamond.

Be on the Lookout
Whenever there is a strange tendency for me to indulge in idleness, the Book of Life bears what may become the tragic imprints of such dangerous doodling.

Substance or Sound
For the solid bark of a thick tree—not the jarring bark of a dog—is far more substantive, more resilient, and more durable.

The Relentless Movement of Time

[I]
Time is blooming bomb, moving steadily;
It moves secretly, sounding under deep dark and desolate tunnels;
It ticks persistently inside the thick tight trunk of an accelerating red Corvette.
Oh Yes! Someone detects its prophetic click inside a clear cellar of a castle.

[II]
Time is an incessant stream wearing away an emerald;
At first the green marble stone has a sparkling shine;
Yet the persistent and constant yearly rubbing of the stream on the gem's surface causes it to decay;
Phenomenally, the water's waves fluctuate back and forth against the declining stone thereby producing the offspring of age.

[III]
Oh! Discover the meaning of time through the rising and setting of the sun.
Little by little the twilight of the cool dawn gives way to the crisp bright cloudless day;
Watch! As the sun throws off its preeminent brilliance, generating a glittering array of golden lilies, cerulean grass, and luminous oakwood trees;
Yet in each human glimpse the scintillating sun takes its gradual journey.

[IV]

Time measures the sound of the human heartbeat. Hear the increased rhythmic oscillation that will again as tormented soldiers run toward the nearest pounding ditch. *Ba...Boom! Ba...Boom!* They seek a hopeful refuge away from their perceived enemies.

Therein exist heightened adrenaline and developing sweat among the haggard soldiers. Most importantly, the emaciated soldiers' hearts palpitate toward the rhythmic drumbeat of eternity. Their envisioned opponents release bombers from the sky, bringing destruction upon the dreaded human figures huddled inside the small German foxhole. Alas—a misuse of time. Grabs!...Groans!...A stifling humanity of graceless geniuses. Therefore, much great potential do not burst from their creative chrysalis to brilliance. Brilliance, however, without conscience is like the planets without the sun! Ours is a world of wayward bull moose uproaring in a forest of a million midnights. Or ours is a world of uproaring monkeys that burst in dark, drenched dungeons? Or ours is a world of awakening roaches that rumble at oceanic depths of the dark earth.

With glum and gloom, an onlooker reads from the tombstone's epitaph:

His corpse now belongs to the residues of civilization...
For the plea of time passed them by;
The plagues of war raised their cry;
The unfading shadows of eternity—no one can deny;

Though humanity moans and sighs for relief, the present moment forges ahead through the throng of cheerless song. Our heartbeat cannot repeat the history of life's symphony...herein the pulsation of the human heart lies an irresistible measurement in time that must ultimately shift its small connecting wheels toward the giant Gangetic entity of eternity.

A Complex Human Circle

[I]
Around and around this complex human sphere;
Revolves an amalgam of radiant yellow, choleric red, and despondent black;
Therein, within the rich rotunda at the New York Botanical Garden, are ripened rhododendrons, fresh rhubarb, and the surrounding chuckles of the jaybirds.
A sweet joy is found in the tinted spring.
Likewise, the human disposition cycles around the springtime warmth of radiant cheerfulness. Such exuberant glee and illuminating ecstasy emerge as Goya and Haku finally meet their glorious day in the joy bells of a Wedding.
The gentle laughter of the newborn and the onrushing happiness of the wedded family and friends express the dynamic human cycle of jubilee.

[II]
Around and around, the sun ushers the earth into a scorching summer in St. James, Barbados. A swarm of bees encircle a banana tree, flying toward the syrup of a snow comb found in Jack's hand. The sizzling heat ascends from the outer roof of the yellow chalet cart. The small network of workers—with their safari hats—pick the sugar canes. The sizzling heat causes an ache to their heads and sweat upon their brows. What searing heat, relieved perhaps only by a tropical storm!

Similarly, the human mood anchors around a passionate or irascible point.

An enraged Jack murders Ted in the streets of Harlem without any justification.

Jack's excuse is that Ted kept looking at him. Pressed by boiling anger,

Jack pulls out a pistol, firing a bullet inside Ted's chest. On the color screen of his mind, Jack sees an unlit white candle and a bloody dagger. As a psychopath, this one case sparks the flame of his heated madness. Inflamed in his folly, at age 19, Jack burns his father and cuts the limbs of his mother in a procrustean format. Indeed the heated drama is no melodrama, but it is a spectacular arrangement of human fusion vented on the offal stages of Harlem. It is the sign of the volatile feelings of the youth who seethe their venom in flame.

[III]
Inexorably, the axial rotation of the earth ushers in an austere winter in Salem Massachusetts. Cirrus clouds stretch over the huge Gothic Cathedral of St. Martha. Unadorned crows and hawks shiver in the bare, blistering winds. The treks vanish leading toward the Cathedral's thick black door. A strange medley of hollow howl and a snowy avalanche fracture the bones of three squirrels left for dead. Two desperate hunters—wrapped in thick black trench coats—grab the three dead squirrels placing them in their small black sack. In the frigid night, the black hooded rash hunters heat the squirrels in an iron bowl above a blazing flame. Thinking they are John Montague, they dine upon slices of squirrels between two pieces of toasted bread.

Along the west Charles Bridge, estranged nomadic figures drag upon the land parallel to the frozen Creek River. Upon the stiff necks of these neglected vagabonds are written: Gloom, Dejection, or Neglect. Pale from the long night of bitterness, their unwashed hands fumble through barrels for food. Neglected Jack mutters undetected words then mentions in vernacular English, "I'm a hungry, depressed and been neglected for years!" Frozen Mack decries, "I'm a long way from home, but this bitter experience shows no comfort of ever getting back home." In an existential mood, Jonathan concludes, "I hate life and life hates me." Herein as the season's cycles, the human feelings revolve around an axis of gloominess, dejection, or neglect.

Just as the earth whirls or spins around the sun producing a kaleidoscope of weather patterns, so do humans spin—usually around events—producing a chain reaction of moods, feelings, or dispositions. Based upon heredity, past experience humans can be predisposed to any one of these moods. Their reaction to the event is what produces the response or mood. Some are sanguine; some are irascible; some are even melancholy. Yet these shifting moods make up the huge Ferris wheel of the complex human cycle.

Without Armor

Part I

As if sprawled on a bleak alley—mentally deranged yet muscle bound;
Though Herculean art—art thou without armor?
Thou trampled the gargantuan sea monster;
Now thou art a trampled tramper;
Thy heyday has turned into a sullen day;
No arctic blast could revitalize thee;
Only that strange paradoxical sword that mends the languid heart
into a limpid one:

Part II

Far spun glib as a shield for the street hustle;
Run ready run swing as a parvenu;
Flung farfetched toward the field of human blue;
Spineless yet portraying backbone;
Marrow less yet portraying substance;
Brainless yet displaying compelling brain power;
Without Armor!
Without Armor!

A scan... A slam...
A sham
Starless spangles and
Bannerless
Yet a cutthroat seeking to strangle the elderly in the village;
Raising a causeless mutiny in any town.
Producing a raid in the dreadful slums and ghettos of our city.
Is this glazing armor or is this tawdry artillery?

Quest for Manhood and Peace

I

A lonesome road, I said;
A never-ending path freshly led;
When I walk through the desert, fear rushes my heart;
An anticipation of danger reminding me where I am from the start;
Oh! Lad with weary feet and heavy hands and with a restless soul
while
traveling to *the Unseen Promised Land.*

II

Each assertive stride builds a level of pride;
I cannot hide; I must continue reaching the other side; restless winds
whip through the thick sands causing the bright atmosphere to
become
blurry;
"I must reach that Ancient Landmark, "I say, progressing with hurry;
Oh! Lad with weary feet and heavy hands and with a restless soul
while
traveling to *the Unseen Promised Land.*

III

Like pilgrims and strangers, I view the mainland thus swimming the
shores
for the very first time;
While those brilliant stars guide me from the dark desert land into
a place
of sunshine;

That brilliant ball of fire slowly arises from the eastern horizon like a glowing
phoenix gradually ascending from its ashes;
Yet I am a traveling chap who swims the turbulent shores while in sudden
clashes;

IV

With continuous tides, the shores roar with whirlwinds of anger;
Seeking to discourage me from confronting this current danger;
Though my body is frail from the troubling winds of calamity;
I must affirm my manhood without losing my sanity;
When I began this initiation process, I knew that I would face troublesome tests;
Now the shaky ground of my manhood is firm without inward shouts of protests;
For the storms of life add stature to my personhood;
As the blue meridian winks its gigantic eye at him with its celestial brightness;
Raising himself away from the heavy waters suddenly he collapses into the great bosom of the land he sought so desperately after;
A land replete with rest, tranquility, and an outpouring of laughter;
Once a young boy searching for a haven of joyful release,
Now a young man resting in *the Unseen Promised Land* of fulfilling peace.
Oh! How he once was a lad with weary feet, heavy hands, and a restless soul, but now a full-grown man finding *the Unseen Land*, keeping his soul perfected.

The Folly of Fame

(The Trap of the Fool's Cap)

As you may not know, a man from Notre Dame had a folly in fame;
Sir James Henry Nuton was his proverbial name;
Who would frolic as he pranced life's forbiddance to proclaim?
How great am I to gallop and gamble through the Garden Grove in sweeping rain;
Acute and astute as the musicians played the flute,
Nuton sailed through the Fabulous Halls of Fame;
In his misconstrued debut entitled, *"The Figurehead in Fluke"*
James dramatized the futility of fame;
Prince Whales sailed smoothly through the political shores with no shame and fame;
To this hour;
No realized power;
For he devoured;
By the most delicate passion flower;
Instead he was a folly figurehead;
In dread;
Who was led;
By his noble siblings through unfathomable power;
Yes just a figurehead instead;
With false fame that is dead;
With no true power said;
The acclaimed actor;
Then the floodgates opened and yea the waters gashing and dashing came;
A sad somber, silly reminiscent soliloquy of how the foaming frolicking frog formed his pseudo-fame.

A Valley in the Alley

Oh! How disheartening. I see a bleak vulnerable valley in the aching alley; vestal verdure does not even exist—just thorns or thistles. Ouch! Ouch! Ouch! I see a sharp, sullen, and Saturnine existence. Boy! Those thistles began to grow and magnify with their showy, prickly heads.

A decrepit man moves sluggishly in the dim and dingy alley casting a shadow upon the alley's fetid, foul dumpster. The pale phantoms of his life harrowed Donald with persistent job denial and haunted him with the blight of doubt and fear. His hair is in locks of wool and his body is sadly clad in musty drapes with shredded molded military boots. He was a general with the military during World War II. Donald's life was not one of awe, but one replete with austerity. He was born without a father. He worked with mom and children in the sweltering Mississippi fields. His confiding male emblem: Big Babe Ruth! Yes the urban blight of Southwest Georgia and Northeast New York portray any untold shrubs found inside cubbyholes, ditches, tunnels, and bypasses.

Another dependent man draws himself from a sully drain as a slimy placid pale python easing from the thick grass. He wears a tawdry chain with a foul smelling long sleeve shirt and a sudden stench comes from his shredded undergarments as if a plethora of skunks emitted their scent at the San Francisco Oakland bay. Suddenly two muscle-bound men walk toward the direction of the manhole. Foul Flatworms Freddy creeps back into the dark hole where his life is now temporarily shut from the public domain. Not even a photographer or news reporter could capture the unheard flatland of the sewage.

Only the common Joe blow of the agonizing alley could pinpoint the urban surrounding to its fine flash points. As Joe Blow looks out the window of his house, he sees a seventy-one-year-old man who shoots a seventeen-year-old man in the chest. Yes, this tragic, trifling incident occurs in the dark alley of Harlem New York. The boy is left for dead and the pale corpse oozes blood from the chest into the veins of cracks of the street. If there were even a flat-water course to refresh these parched plants, it would ease the pain of human suffering found in the Valley of the Alley.

In the twilight of the night a vesper sparrow rests upon an almond tree. Its pensive stare suggests a yearning for the golden dew of hope and motivation to refresh the dinky shrubs found inside of the hubbub ditches of America. Who will provide an oasis to invigorate the sizzling dregs of humanity?

Surviving in Patience

Panic is a delicate bubble that shakes and breaks with the boisterous winds.
So you rehearse… "Oh no! I'm about to burst." Patience, however, fastens
that fragile bubble, thereby strengthening its thin walls with impenetrable
depths of durability. So you say plausibly, "I'm going to contain myself
during life's awe-inspiring trilogy.
Panic outbursts, patience firmly holds; Panic brings blurs, patience
crystallizes; Panic consumes, patience conserves; Panic enrages, patience
calms; Panic is fearful, patience is faithful; Panic enslaves, patience saves.
Patience provides enough resilient glue to satisfy humanities burning desire
for survival.
Patience is that tsunami survivor who, amid the raging storm, embraces the
tree and hence glues together a remarkable episode of courage.
Patience is also that spectacular glue reconciling decade-long family feuds.
Patience is, of course, found in that struggling student who week after week
grapples with algebra problems and then finally glues together a coherent
method to master algebra.

Patience is for sure found in that self-conscious mortal who under constant
self-evaluation grows weak and weary, then glues together a solid network
of praise thereby rescuing him from the ravages of defeat.
Patience is finally found in that precious mortal who is scoffed and ridiculed
and who though thick glue that person's composure is held together void
of neither animosity nor vengeance. Yes, patience is one of those special human
survival kits that preserve the human soul's tapestry rather than destroy it.

Have You Been There?

Don't be taken aback by the brunt of life's heavy sack;
You say:
In disarray;
Fused with futile furry;
Gagged in a circle not to assuage my pain—you hurry;
Like an unsympathetic bloodhound;
You're bound;
Trying to blunder through my day;
You fuss and you bluster with a blow-by-blow blunderbuss along my way;
Bombarded, bobbed, and almost boggled, a voice bolsters my shaky hut by
saying assuredly, "Do not fear!"
Do not be downcast or howled, but hunker humbly at the hump, "For I've
been there!"

Oh! How You Speak

Your powerful baritone voice resounds from the rostrum of the Ralph J.
Bunche Elementary School.
Your all-encompassing topic: "The Impossible Dream."
Oh! How you speak with such a demanding thunderous appeal and
your
dynamic words: "Don't give up! cause a flash of chills within my
being. Then I begin to sneeze and squeeze the loose wooden
handle on the
dilapidated assembly chair.
I'm captivated by your eloquent sincerity.
I'm captivated by your uncanny capacity to compel me to do my
best.
When I hear your resonant voice, I feel destined to achieve greatness.
When I hear your resounding voice, I see an erupting volcano pause
in its
course.
When I hear your conciliatory voice, I think of philosophical
differences
understood and appreciated.
When I hear your stentorian voice, I hear a rolling stream that inces-
santly splashes
over rocks then congeals.
When I hear your melodious voice, it's a soothing ointment that
seeks to heal
the bruised branches of oppression.
Your sincere voice is loud and clear as its vocal cords grip the very
corridor of my
heart.

Your compassionate voice reaches the young and the old.
The honest tone found in your smooth voice is the sincere volume of the
heart, raised for your attentive audience to hear clearly and respond freely
with open dialogue.
The homespun language and the dynamic rhythm cause some people to
respond with sorrow and others with laughter.
Oh! Your sweet, sincere baritone voice is a harmonic masterpiece thereby
evoking the bundled feelings of my fragile heart.
Your booming, blooming voice is one of exhilaration and expectation.

Your Vital Ear

Your vital ear is displayed vividly as you sit by a despondent and bereaved Aunt Sally Jones, who is devastated by the disturbing death of her husband, Daniel Jones, who was killed in a green Honda Accord at the scene in Oak County.

You tune intently and gladly into her weary moans and groans. Instead of hastily replying that you understand her poignant pain, your fixed stare serves soothingly as an ointment to her aching heart as she senses strongly your ardent feelings of love and affection toward her without you uttering a single word to her.

Your shared experience of witnessing the death of your parents, who were killed by a drive-by shooting on Hill Drive, is enough to identify with Sally's deep hurt, devastating sorrow, and shattered hope.

You're attentive toward a howling man, Terry Brown, who pouts and shouts about his painful current economic condition in Memphis, Tennessee.

You say not a single word to him, but you identify with his outpouring of surging outcries.

You discover that perhaps his profound wound of neglect is largely inexpressible, and thus he has huge deposits of inner turmoil coiled up inside of him that is about to unravel.

Terry finally verifies your impressions that he is indeed deeply hurt from his chaotic past by mentioning, "I'm sick and tired of overwork and underpay. I feel deeply humiliated."

Your vital ear is open toward a crestfallen Mary Maker, who was jilted by a jeering John Campbell.

Your vital ear serves perpetually as an extrasensory organ that listens to the full content of Mary's incessant wail and throb.

You know the timely when to comfort her and promptly when to leave her alone at the royal red Norwegian Palace found inside her luxuriously spacious antechamber.

Oh! How you listen with magnanimity to the universal fainted cries and woes of withering human configurations expressing, "Show compassion; I'm human," while they virtually vanish beside New York's gigantic rectilinear buildings, Japan's colossal automatons, and by way of worldwide commercialism.

Oh! How you listen to the sweet whispers of amicability between Joe and Karen as they skip gladly and sing sweet love songs toward one another along the Serene English Channel.

Wow! Your keen ear penetrates through the desolate dark dungeons of Spain and hears the humming sounds of a small red dragonfly.

Amazingly, your excellent ear pierces through the great chambers of Southern Italy and hears the jerking movement of a grayish brown jerboa.

Oh! How you hear the brown deaths head moth sound its vanishing buzz in scorching Death Valley.

Surprisingly, you hear the distant maiden with pinkish white adornment found in the flourishing meadows of Dalton Georgia churning milk used to produce butter.

Astoundingly, your wonderful ear regularly prepares your receptive ear and mind for a thoughtful and kind word to share with others by carefully registering their thoughts and feelings into your very own chemistry.

You voluntarily pull yourself temporarily into their distinctive circumference and thereby merge within their revolving sphere of seething thoughts and emotions. Indeed, your enthusiastic attentiveness is monumental. With it, the fragile and shadowy outcries of mankind would remain merely

as a horrible heap of cold cadavers found floating aimlessly inside the reputable Nile River, soon found by desperate and distant anthropologists. Later these distant anthropologists schedule the chillsome cadavers for dissection that will involve criticism or analysis rather than genuine affection or acknowledgement. Hence, otherwise detached spectators neglect animate Kings or Queens unceasingly.

Yet your vital ear resurrects "the living dead" and makes known their unheard petitions.

Your Vital Voice

Your vital voice gives hope to your lovely wife, who has a tiresome day, and you say, "Come on, honey; you will make it." So she succumbs to your soothing words of encouragement.

Your vital voice gives hope toward your wonderful husband, who is fatigued by life's disappointments, and you say, "Honey don't give up you will make it." So he succumbs to your soothing words of encouragement.

Your vital voice injects significance into your children's minds, and when they become adults, they love and cherish the timeless principles that you've instilled in them and the irreplaceable inspiration you imparted to them.

Your vital voice is a significant force that draws the attention of Jackie who is about to jump from the top of the Empire State Building but she hears your life-giving words and suddenly changes her mind. She seeks to receive help for a transformation in her life.

Your vital voice is a significant force that gains the attention of a dying Bettie who, at Grady Memorial Hospital, lies supine with the nagging disease of lung cancer and your prompt vigorous and humorous words are channeled toward sick Bettie thus uplifting her spirit and she begins to smile with an outpouring of remarkable zest.

Your vital voice is an important force that, once imparted, touches the lonely heart of Mrs. Jones, who asks you to return and visit her while she sits secluded at Springfield Memorial Nursing Home. Your inspiring words give Mrs. Jones the reason to find meaning in life. She thanks you for your kind words that uplift her personhood.

Yes, *your vital voice* is a torch of light to millions of people who feel voiceless and thereby cringe into the dark, dirty ditches of despair.

You hear their countless sufferings and henceforth become their vital mouthpiece.

You're the resurging spring breeze that breathes new life into the tender orchids found in the plain lands of Georgia, Carolinas, and Mississippi.

You're the rekindling spring breeze that restores life into the withering lilies of Oklahoma, Minnesota, and Idaho.

You're the vibrant spring wind that breathes life upon the precious grape vines of Virginia, thereby causing them not to recoil in fear and despair but to blossom and bloom into a splendid stronghold.

You make the philodendrons spring and sing.

You make the Poinsettias sprout and shout.

You make the spotted owl neither howl nor growl, but rather sail and hail.

You're the vital standing stone in your own home with brilliant starlight providing a lucid path for your domestic steamboat and for all other local, national, and international steamboats.

You give staying power to every royal lily, rubber plant, and royal palm that would otherwise smother in a stifling steam chest.

Your *vital voice* and choice reach not only to America, but also to the world.

Your *vital voice* makes life more livable, more endurable, and more exportable.

Without it many people would perpetually blister and bleed.

With it many people see your timeless fluorescence emanating from the lovely lotus found upon the fertile soils of southern Asia.

You're an Unforgotten Symphony

As the dark cloud rolls back and the radiant sun hastens to brighten your day,

Indeed you're an unforgotten symphony developing into a magnificent prelude, thus introducing the timeless theme of humility.

As the royal red curtains are rolled back and God beckons you to reckon with Him, your soliloquy is indeed that of contrition in His sight, not your own.

Indeed, you're an unforgettable symphony that summons ringing joy bells throughout time and eternity.

As you walk toward the center of the stage and the spotlight shines upon you, your primary concern regarding that piercing light is that it uproots any remaining thick layers of rooted soil in you, thereby implanting a free flowing projected symphony that is not muffled by any self-inflicted defects.

In a sense, you're an unforgotten symphony because you're a forgotten symphony in the eyes of God, who shines behind and beyond the Grampian Mountains of Scotland and the Great Smoky Mountains of the United States.

When you climax into that spectacular note leading toward the epilogue, the Great Stage Actor of Life will pause and think that "the best symphony is one's life and legacy in the eyes of the almighty, and your life rings out in needful and noble proportions in His sight."

For you're not a nightmare to the frail world, but a special nightingale soaring into the dim, misty sky, thus introducing new meaning into the base, alto, and soprano chords—even after death!

Ode to the Sun

Oh sun! How you shine your lovely rays of light?
Covering me with your warmth and brightness;
Please give me the key that locks up night!
Shining like the divine hosts of righteousness;
Transforming the bleakness of man's wretched state;
Oh! How you penetrate the earth's dampness?
Ruling out evil's entire fate;
Being my guiding light amid the water's rage;
Bringing hope throughout every age;
Projecting luminous light across your crested cosmic page;
And then sweetly you move toward a long, joyous daybreak.

A Sunlit Heart

Along the fleeting way of time and tide;
The moon's celestial shadow passes gradually by;
Shrinking considerably as the piercing sun's splendor from the blissful crystal blue sky;
Suffusing into the spectacularly huge and gloriously awakened tranquil Arctic Ocean tide;
At once the rumbling, roaring waves of the sea did ache and sigh;
At once the sagging magnolia and maple flowers revive and arise
From that sullen deep cry;
While thy drooping heart awakens gladly to fly;
From its former chrysalis of despair, left sadly to die;
Wonderfully, torment is transmuted into a thick row of cotton obliterated by the magnificent sun's crisp morning golden rays;
Joyfully, despair is transmuted into a silver maple leaf drifting on the gusty winds, as thou proclaim an electrified hurray;
Any hillcrest of burden is suddenly rolled away, forgotten, into the Red Sea;
Neither returning to thee at whim, nor at will haunting thee;
Neither a mortal feat, nor a frail drumbeat;
Nor for that matter any finite auxiliary;
Only Divine Benevolence supports diffusing the gloomy cloud heads that loom;
Turning them into a brilliant sunrise while being in bliss and in good company inside the Glowing upper room;
Christ, the Champion, the cheer-upper, the consoler—all in one and more;
Thou keep smiling in reassurance of His gleeful gaze;

For He is kind, peaceable, pleasant, companionable, neighborly, and sympathetic—now and forevermore;
Though the sullen shades were down;
And once dragged the rugged ground;
Now thou art no longer plunged, drowning fearfully into a huge splintering sea of despair;
Twisted, nagged, or harrowed by the sea serpent of fear;
For a Divine cosmic ray now illuminates thy habitation with a sweet solace, treasured admiration, and a heart replete with glorious grace;
Once thrust despairingly underground, you now transcend resiliently the stern ground, indebted to the One placing a nimbus surrounding thy face;
Once sheltered inside of a bleak chamber beleaguered by daggers of overwhelming dread and increasing sorrow;
Now thou reside inside of a divinely gorgeous pavilion, glancing at a brilliantly sunlit today and tomorrow.

A River Turning Toward the Dawning Light

A river I still see that twists then finally turns toward the dawning light:
This magnificent but firm overflow is largely steady, though at times it pushes and splashes into a surprising trickling course;
A glittering crystal-blue river I still see, wherein the overflowing joy, heartfelt laughter, and sincere smiles of my friends remain as a perpetual onrush—never fading.
An abiding waterway I see, wherein a vicarious sacrifice is made through the Good Shepherd as He bears the toils, hardships, and disappointments of nearby pilgrims and the whole world.
For the poignancy of such a grave sacrifice is felt as though the piercing, indiscriminate heat beats and swells against my frail skin.
A special flowing river wherein I hear the quintessence of Divine Love harmoniously ringing forth in bass, treble, soprano, and alto, even through the desultory movements of the drone, the seagull, and the dabbling duck, His cosmic melody is carried toward the steady flight of the dove, the sparrow, and the eagle.
This monumental river in which I continue to rest and bathe presents a pure taste to my senses as it soothes and replenishes my insatiable appetite.
The serene, pearly-water brings to mind the inescapable taste of cinnamon, the endless bite of chocolate almond, and the unending flavor of maple peanut butter.
Once again, I feel and rest upon this plush blue-river, and it reminds me of an ancient golden basin housing only a drop from its huge watershed.

The remaining braided river flows inexorably toward the dawning of
a brighter, better day.
For neither mortal man nor beast can cause the narrow river to sway;
While they all stand in awe, moving suddenly out of its way.
Each splendid onrush flows gaily and triumphantly into the out-stretched arm of the sun's rays;
Indeed, this is not an ordinary water flow… for it is "a gorgeous river turning toward the dawning day."

The Withered Leaf

One day in the quiescent Appalachian Mountains, there grew a magnificent raspberry tree, springing to a prodigious height;
Every creature from the tiger, the red fox, and the Newfoundland dog lodged under the huge tree for protection from the scorching sun.
This distinguished tree almost demanded the attention of the lofty mountains, for it was a rather amazing sight;
But upon the arid ground of Appalachian area, by lovely tree, stood a withered leaf whose growing saplessness was not fun;
Surely enough, there stood the dried-up leaf—crispy, cold, and compressed,
Void of any sweet moisture circulating to the nearby homestead;
Will this crispy brown unadorned leaf arise from its pathetic dryness?
Or will it remain a sorrowful number left smudged upon the stale grounds of helplessness;
Awake, dejected leaf, for my hometown needs you;
Arise from your prune-like condition, producing new dew;
Who, you?
Yes, you!
Help replenish the parched soils of the thick-bodied earth;
And thus gladly rehearse that this is no ordinary birth;
Thereby causing every other leaf to spring from dearth to mirth;

The Rejuvenating Flower

Once upon a time in the balmy Colorado Desert, there developed a whirlwind;
That tempest tossed a greenish white flower from a Joshua tree upon the ruffled sand.
Surrounding the bright flower, there were short, shriveled, and dried leaves that swirled in wind;
For they produced discordant sounds as if coming from a mad marching band close at hand;
Or a joust in the wind made with a host of knights with lances in combat;
Or a flock of magpies chattering noisily to dismantle any lingering straps;
Yet this greenish white flower radiated warmth and brilliance upon the Colorado desert.
Wherein the gigantic gust of wind ceased and once more quiescence overtook the dejected earth;
Indeed, the highly precious flower served as a marvelous mother of pearl, awakening the scorched leaf into a striking new birth;
From a solemn scowl to a jovial sunrise;
All the wait was worthwhile;
The splendid Colorado desert has reached a perennial smile;
See what difference one live flower can make upon a desert field of parched leaves;
There's an aliveness of authentic wonder or thrill far beyond what any mortal believes;

The Maple Leaf

In the heart of Boston, Massachusetts, there is a maple leaf;
Separated from other leaves as a "fare thee well";
Beyond questionable fantasy, the combined scent of samaras exudes from the thick wreath;
A grab-bag man tried to smother the sweet, splendid scent, yet he fell,
Falling feet first into the water, with a flaw in character revealed as a feet of clay;
Yet a warm feeling exists; inhabitants inhale vigorously that marvelous, soothing maple sap near Chestnut Bay;
Wow, a lovely smell that cuddles cuckoos and California condors together;
A sweet, awakening aroma flourishes as fresh daffodils croon in the crisp spring weather;
A special dandelion with a superb fragrance enhances any mortal's salad for the better;
Fresh meadows gloriously sing with red robins, and clusters of bees pull to the honeycomb of thy succulent sweetness;
A fabulous fresh spring delight, as juicy as roseberries and scrumptious raspberries, harmonize humans with thou and their surroundings;
Every time that thou art around, I not only see thy substantial sweetness,
But I also feel thee as being a part of life's best;
Treasure as a special cinnamon balm soothing my stomach as I am running.
You are a refreshing breeze of maple-pine scent brushing gently upon the tip of my sweaty nose on a scorching summer day;

Yes, the maple leaf brings out its very best when every mortal being is gently touched, awakened, renewed, and refreshed by thy all-encompassing sway;
This magnificent maple leaf is a part of thee especially when thou art embodied with its noble characteristics of sweetness and light;
Sweet potato, sweet pepper, sweet-sap, and sweetmeat also serve as a great bite for a prodigious appetite;
Yet thy magnolia interior underpins a very strong but precious sight;
Oh! Maple leaf from the big apple tree, thou art stronger than any mortal with muscular might;
Stretch forth thy perennial sweetness unto the heavens, thereby reaching fresh, unforeseen, and incredible heights;
Oh! Delicate maple leaf, we are depending upon You;
To permeate your unparalleled fragrance unto the barren lands with a sparkling fresh morning dew;
Thereby producing a beautiful line of lilies in the valley;
And a radiant row of sunflowers in the alley;
You bring out the best in the vast vestige of America and the surrounding world;
You are the special sweet seed which every discordant heart and mind magnificently blends into a harmonious swirl;

Undaunted Truth Yet Adorning Forever

In a spectacular land far reaching, lies and half-truths dazzle within the solemn, thick fog of the night; however, truth is unadorned, earnest, and persistent in her rugged passage;

In a huge theater of shallow amusements, truth is neglected, bruised, and snubbed toward the bristling grounds, but she shall someday arise and shed forth precious mercy on the crusted grounds;

Like junk, men cast her into the trash, unto the waters as mere jetsam, thereby sinking to the very base of the frigid forest, but in the thick mist of the solemn night, termites of gold prick at their wooden hearts, and hence the blistering winds roar and soar to great heights. While others are daunted, truth continues her arduous journey amid countless opposition.

In the world of academia, great and noble men apostatize; but too often, their "phenomenal ideas" get more recognition or praise than the unwavering beam of truth that radiates with joy in spite of the pounding, bleak tides of opposition.

Men may, like vicious tuataras, spew out fiery spears of hate and plan the most notorious conspiracies; but in a flash and thunderclap, truth is a thunderbolt obliterating the egregious deeds of mankind into infinitesimal pieces;

Henceforth and forever, palpable truth glows with all of its luminous and royal apparel, including its diadem and rod, all transcending into an unthinkable realm of prominence.

By many it is unmarred, but in a trod path of a remnant, it towers in striking sincerity, noble character, and powerful utterance. Who can deny truth's paradoxically painful and joyful tendencies, along with its revealing presence, especially when it's etched in the hearts and minds of dedicated and genuine pilgrims who uphold it unflinchingly?

Oh! Barren Land Shine

Oh! Barren Land… shine! Thy crisp roots art withered, and thy loose ribs art old strips torn by living winds of oppression and neglect;
Thou, shallow ground, art impervious, and thy vast expanse is in dread of wholesome purity;
Through ruin's gash into the pitiful, prunelike roots, replenish the waters that awaken
Thy bleached valleys.
Oh! The depth of this perpetual famine is rather astonishing;
Even if thou shouldst wail from thy dry, deep depths, that would let me know that thou acknowledgest thy drought, indeed, thou art a mammoth cavity void of vital torrents replenishing thy gap.
For thou art now a cold crusty clay, but think thou art a soft, lavish pillow of soil—fertile and ready for corn, peas, and collard greens;
Nevertheless, thy distressed earth contains a heap of corpses producing a foul oozing odor mounting to gross proportions.
It is a boundless horror for any living mortal to witness.
The crows cross, crowing thy land in distress; then in suspense, they wait to prey on the dingy dead bodies found half-buried in thy sullen opening.
Thou art dirty, dingy, and dim, thus swerving away from the path of incandescent light, thereby becoming a sloth that prowls and growls while further sinking into the swamplands of stagnation.
Oh! Barren Land…Shine from thy long, long, drought and long arid route.

Oh! Barren Land with dried and blistered ribs, this is no place for thee, for thou art to once again radiate brilliance into every place and space throughout thy dim horizon.
A change for the downpour of rain will once more make thy land grow and thereby become fertile…now precious with a never-ending abundance
As if plucked up from the earth, the fresh, mighty torrents penetrate the earthen heart into a new, special design seeded and crafted by the Maker for any inhabitants who plod and plow her creased clay.
For a solemn day is transformed into a gleeful day, for thy native dry land has
been resurrected along the meandering way…into lavished peanut butter
cream cups—sweet and magnificently bright—and far…far from decay!
So, land that is plentiful and free, stretch forth thy bosoms into the far-reaching, transcendent bay.
Oh! Thick land, shine perpetually, even beyond the sinking soap suds of evanescent life and time.

A Mirror and Yet Can't See the Real Me

A mirror—and yet I can't see the real me;
I stare and see a glare of fair beauty.
Yet is that what I see?
Or is it a narcissism through which I see myself as Napoleon on a killing spree;
Yes, a distorted image in which I see myself;
A mirror—and yet I can't see the real me;
I stare and imagine myself as a dazzling prince of charm, who is refined
and seated in the most plush seat, looking up at a fan tracery while inside a
remote Scandinavian palace;
I stare and imagine myself with thick double-layered red silk garments of
beauty—the mirror itself becomes a vain veil where I transfer my thoughts,
viewing futile, superficial beauty; but beneath the veneer, there's malice;
Beneath the veneer, there's a callous heart—a vicious vampire lurking
beneath a Salem, Massachusetts cottage;
A maverick reptilian image the red ooze at thy shoulders in flaming rage;
A hapless hippopotamus tipped and tossed inside a glamorous showboat on
a sensational stage;

Where my brilliant display of fireworks suddenly ceases, thereby making me
a shaded footnote that only when probed, I'm found idly standing at the
bottom of the historical page;
Dost I now see that my daylight hours on earth art scant?
To my great awakening, I'm parched in the piercing sunlight as that
withering plant;
Take one of my leaves—crispy, falling into the baked, brittle clay;
Where all of the delusional streams end the course of my "hit parade;"
And now I'm cast in the midst of the shadows, far away from the
invigorating shade;
Whirling as jumbo jetsam suddenly drifting into the turbulent water of
the Everglades;
No spades;
Or lemonade;
But I now start to see the real me;
In dark, dangling debris;
A fine-tuned mirror—and yes, I'm now beginning to see the real me.

The Insider

Amazingly, the insider probes into my cerebrum as a telescope, detecting the very cells of my skin.

Hence, my thoughts unravel before Him as I walk inside a peaceful pavilion.

As I sing and walk inside a crowded corridor, the insider also chuckles and confidentially shares with me that presently I have quirks of a sanguine disposition. Through His telescope, the huge, dark thunderheads that once existed through moroseness has long dissipated, but there are still infinitesimal strands of darkness and dreariness that yet echo inside the fragile tunnel of my mind, which will soon conspire into a consolidated force. This could place me in an abyss of disappointment and dejection if the twisted cables remain unchecked.

Nevertheless, the insider assures me that through honest probes and consultation with Him, the lingering strands will soon be combated through faith and obedience in Him, and a renewing hope of a brighter day in view. This will at once destroy the gloomy strands through a victorious band, thereby plunging them into the abysmal sand.

Unflickering Flame

Oh! Unflickering flame, continue to shine incandescently throughout the thick region of the solemn night;

Never let thy brilliant glow sadly dash like a frail meteorite taking a downward flight;

Up and out thou goest with unsurpassable heat blazing through any megalith;

Also springing up as long-lived lava blasting through the now sagging sheer rock of the sullen night.

Yes, thy light beam must shine through the sky tower and sidewall to sift through any surviving rubbish, lifting it from the dark, deep pit;

For the ring-necked pheasant is in awe as it gazes at your remarkable glowing nimbus;

My prevailing wail is that thy magnificent light will permeate through this obscure night and thereby draw the attention of the night hawks as they draw nigh to thee;

Nightcrawlers will see thy luminous outpouring and thereby draw nigh to thee;

Night crawlers and nightingales will encircle thee and then surge in direct response to thy warm brilliancy, thereby draw nigh to thee;

Night ravens will no longer suffer from the long agony and ache of crying, but will pour forth with a flood bank of laughter and thereby draw nigh to thee;

Oh! Unflickering flame, please don't—for one moment—cease that magnificent illumination, but emit thy fabulous light into the immensity of the deep, dark Pacific Ocean.

Displaying a wonderful blaze of chariot-like-campfires projected against the solemn, still water, thus reaching beyond the traveled heights of the red-shouldered hawk and also springing beyond mankind's scientific and intellectual notions.

A Fainting Flame Not to Remain

So long as the hustling winds outdo that fainting flame,
the chances for it to remain are minimized;
So long as its inaudible cry is surpassed by the wails of the Pacific Ocean,
the chances for it to remain are also lessened;
So long as there is no glowing heat generated by its presence, what have we but a stifling stockyard?
Or is it now an ember from its once unfettering fire?
Is it now a dim spark that is incapable of being rekindled?
Is its sparse presence to one day degenerate into a thrashing ash?
So the query looms: "What will become of this fainting flame?"
I'll tell you that someday its fainting spark will develop into an exceptional flame;
Thus, it will have a timeless combustion.
A tour de force amid the high tide;
A reassurance of blazing heat amid the bleak austerity of the frozen Alaskan pond;
Oh! Yes, an emergence of a bright new day with a rushing stream of passion;
So this fainting flame will not remain, but will indeed reinvent the mundane course of history, thereby making its own brand of legacy and achievement inside the gold-trimmed pages of life's history book.

Shining Pearls of Fortitude amid This Ephemeral World

I know that courageous pearls exist and persist beyond the sagging world of cowardice;
Beyond the filthy floodgate of human conformity you stand sharp, facing the sharks of terror or force;
Without a wink, shrink, or blink,
You shine as a beam that is projected against the faint night sky.
Why are the nighthawks—once solid brass—now as melting icebergs, dripping away?
Yes, mere orbs of truth grow fainter and fainter until they become obscure vapors, which are now fanciful ideas or phobias inhabiting and haunting the minds of mortals who remain scattered and suspended by mere rot, like skeletons hanging in shadowy, shabby, and web-infested closets, left for commonality and complacency.
Yes, nothing weaker than a shallow roar denigrated by a languid wind is your means to block and bully your fainting victims!
Nevertheless, the pearls of fortitude force forward progressively,
Without bullwhips to blot out bullies,
Without bull tales to anguish and ache bullies,
Without bull snakes to torture bullies;
But glittering pearls of magnanimity that are far beyond the piercing blades of resentment;
Far beyond huge covered cloaks of dissimulation;
Far beyond dusty couples of bickering and backbiting;

After the whistling winds reside, you are alive and thrive as precious gems that are cut rubies, made and polished from the magnificent rocks found upon the Niagara Falls;
You are jubilant jewels after the stench, smoke, and soot somehow thrust themselves into infinitesimal particles suspended in interstellar space.
A shining pearl of fortitude, though once cast out, has made its way through the trail to prevail and outlast any meteorite of obstacles through your bright starlight;
The milieu was once surrounded by deep, dark obscurity, but your courageous ray penetrates through all the mysteriousness and thereby enters a new threshold of scintillating brightness, whereby your Pearls of fortitude continue to shine incandescently unto yet another remarkable realm of transcendence.

A Rock amid the High Tide

Oh, how I see the ruffling waves rush and flow into a noticeable high
tide time after time:
There are the unassailable winds that go along with the gushing high
tide,
Spurred by the gravitational force of the celestial sun and moon;
Thereby causing the barren earth to quake or shake, and oh! My
heart flutters at the thought: "A high tide so soon at noon!"
Shall the compelling anger and irresistible pain of this raging high
tide ever subside?
Oh! How I hear the nuzzled whips of the whistling wind and now the
soaring high tide comes rushing forth:
Mercilessly scattering the beautiful portrait of a Great Smokey
Mountain land scene into what is now inexpressible pieces, a
shredded puzzle from henceforth to oblivion:
Oh! How I feel the intense heat from the raging tidal waves that clash
as they bring a calamitous shock to the horrified atmosphere, as
the swelling humidity rips through the pores of my fragile skin.
Uncontrollably, the tempo of my horrified heart beats faster
and faster and faster. *Ba-boom…Ba-boom…Ba-boom…*
Human lives, houses, villages, and crops are destroyed at whim.
But I smell the pungent flavor of salt from the ocean as the ascend-
ing tidal waves dash into the thunderheaded clouds, which
surround the dome-like sky; and all the more, the unadorned
shores are softened, almost forming cliffs.
Then suddenly and surprisingly, I see the ruffled high waves recede
into an unspeakable calm that soothes my fatigued mind, and
hence the rhythm of my faint heart throbs slower and slower
and slower. *Ba-boom…Ba-boom…Ba-boom*

Incidentally, a melodious chirp—from a red robin—moves along the steady rock of the ocean's shores, as if the robin is caressed by the rock's unwavering support, even through the high tide.

Here in the middle of this special solid rock remains—still and settled— even after the fierce anger and murmurings of the wind and ocean tide subside.

So I touch the rock and consider its smooth solemnity. My once stiff wrist is now smooth and improved. More importantly, I rest and bathe upon this sweet, silent rock; and as I continually rub it, I receive calm acts of reassurance and fortitude. Love, life, and hope from this vital rock invigorate my frail chemistry.

As a weevil latches to a berry on a shaded fruit tree off the east coast of South Africa and will not release, the rock is unforgettably still there.

As the crocodile grips its mouth into one of the branches of the sugar maple tree found in Ohio and will not release, the rock is unrelentingly still there.

As the soaring bald eagle is unmovable in its flight toward the Appalachian Mountains, the rock is inexhaustibly still there.

For This Hallow Rock will serve as a well spring of hope throughout time's staggering tide, thus transforming life's high tide of the gasping human heartbeat into life's smooth ocean of the peaceful human heart-beat by its remarkably stoic existence—though at times its nobility and stature are incomprehensible.

An Open Fountain

An open fountain pouring forth vigorously with all of its sparkling awe;
Rupturing the trail's womb of chirping Florida scrub in the heart of the dawning morning, this morning more and more;
Upon the bright day of today, the disgruntled king and the discontented pauper are also offered a Better freedom than they found in the obscure days of yore:
A spouting sprinkle here;
A spouting sprinkle there;
A dazzling splash to all who want it;
Come while I sing at the morning spring and thus sip it;
Come while I sing at the morning spring and thus dip in it;
Gushing forth in momentum with sparkling free flows;
Rushing along the sacred channel while the whistling wind blows;
Added drops—from the drop box—fill gradually the crimson bucket from the start.
Wow! This miraculous spring continues to purge and replenish my heart;
Herein I store:
And I—heedless to say—ask for more and more;
From the ragpicker to the well-off—hear ye!
For there's a glorious water supply—come see!
Rinsing, showering, and bathing—him, you, and me;
So I now come and thereby see the snatching manacles released gladly, and they are rescued wonderfully from the flighty sea.

I Seem Forgotten

As a pendulous, bleached skull swinging on a string tied to a Joshua tree branch found upon an Arizona desert, I beckon for a refuge, yet I find none.

Across the vast surface sands the brutal winds whip, producing a swarm of cloudiness, thus casting the atmosphere into a transcendent level of geographical brutality.

More so, the restless winds tease a new dimension of torment and turmoil by driving their piercing gale like a rapid whip drill into the sun's sandy brow.

I beseech thee from a special ship amid a placid Caribbean ocean, where I'm caressed by thy gentle soothing hand and am comforted by thy firm, reassuring voice.

Now, however, I reckon with the precarious winds and ominous clouds that frown hard and unflinchingly. Around me, the colossal riverbanks beset me with an intensified rage and unassailable revenge.

Around me the Atlantic Ocean surges and wails, tempting me to succumb to its contagious roar and its pathetic restlessness.

Around me the redwood trees swing as dangling maroon tubes, but impressively, they are not broken by this unhindered and unseen catastrophe.

From the owl atop the barren shallow creek, there is a nice nightingale waiting for me in glee, thus resting its soft feet upon the splendid redwood tree.

Interestingly enough, the glittering sun in recrudescence emits its special glow rays, an awe-inspiring symmetry, thereby appeasing the bruised and downtrodden earth from its blistered and aching woes.

It is then I realize that I'm not forgotten, but through the boisterous wind, my faith is formed or fashioned into what is designed to become an instrument of extended trust, never-ending dependence, and tireless commitment.

It is then that I must look to the One who places me within a solid cleft, while unexpectedly the looping waves ruffle; and He whispers, "I'm unforgotten."

Distorted Voice

Outside I hear a distorted voice that—sometimes, of course—is inaudible
to the human ear, but is in fact audible to the human heart;
Oh yes! I indeed feel—beyond the multiple symbols of languages and the
myriad of human personalities—your blistering, chilly ache and your all-too-long forgotten anguish as a misunderstood sojourner;
I hear indeed your muffled and distorted voice as it ascends the heaven
of heavens, thereby unleashing a timeless aroma to my nostrils.
So let your voice be distorted upon the earth;
For it will be remembered in heaven;
So let your name be tainted and ridiculed on earth;
For it will be honored and cherished in heaven;
So long as you wait patiently upon Me;
Obey Me;
And honor my Son through your life.

Toward the Helm of Victory

All around, there is the intransigent growl of the fierce and piercing winds,
which refuse constantly to settle from their protruding tongues of feud and
fury;
Magnificent mansions and beautiful houses dwindle into filthy, floppy debris;
According to some dazzled minds of cinema, the moody winds escalate
into a scornful tempest, thereby suddenly turning their surroundings topsy-turvy;
Any remains are snuffed into boisterous seas;
Mankind's think tank will neither formulate a plan to mitigate the seas
nor the trees;
Just then, the Captain of the ship steers the wheel of the ship;
Wonderfully, the whipping winds cease;
An unassailable calm reverberates from my hip to lip;
It is then that I reckon to cherish life's throwdown, with the Captain
assuring me toward the helm of peace;
It is then that I express a hearty hello to the Helper of the ship who made
the winds cease;
Thenceforth, at the helm of many victories is likely the guise of life's raging
tides of perplexity.
So I must see clearly my way through the seething winds and sea—
yes, toward the helm of victory.

Only One Time to Cross

I have only one time to cross;
Am I prepared to make life's journey a feat?
Yes, I have only one time to cross;
I must suffer if I'm distracted in any way and thereby sway from the narrow way;
But once again, I have only one time to cross;
For I must face the agony and ache of conscience if I choose the sweeter
allurement of impulse;
The ceaseless enchantment of foes;
The timeless bewitchments of enemies;
And even sometimes the charted obstacles set by family and friends;
All of which can impede or block a path—to no end.
And so the poignant question that pierces my mind and soul: *"Am I prepared*
to make life's journey a feat?"
A challenging proposition—with only one time I have to cross and thereby
make it to the other side.

Noble Opportunity

A noble opportunity awaits me,
And yet, as in the huge sphere of the gorgeous galaxy, there are the
astronomical planets and the bright stars that gird interstellar space, floating
into my ken as bright, sparkling gems,
These gems cause me to stand stupefied while cleaving to the twinkling
image of life's manifold allurements.
To a degree, there is an admixture of joy, anxiety, laughter, and even
disappointment once I imbibe these trinkets.
As before the crimson sky, there is a motley of conspicuous apparel and flashy
vehicles, along with the ephemeral glitter of stellar parties and starlight
entertainments—all of which remain as flimsy moss absorbed by the ocean. Then there is the further churning of the ocean's push and pull, thus
engrossing the scum into an infinitesimal existence.
Then there is a strange pause of silence. Thereafter, the rushing winds
whip as if to suggest to me the irrelevance of such clumps of moss through
the incessant howls, and so the scum drifts quickly from me into the waters
of oblivion.
Amid the huge strands of shallowness or emptiness, a noble opportunity
leaves before me a splendid vernal grove, wherein a glittering path awaits

me to walk therein and hence inhale the invigorating air of joy or fulfillment,
void of transient hopes. What course shall I decide to take? Let me choose
freely the noble opportunity and thereby awake into an eternal and hopeful
fate.

One Step Further

Just one unhesitant step further makes all the difference in the world—I
must not yield.
A solemn step moving closer toward the victory field;
Just one united step further through the fiery flame once again not to
yield;
A firm step forward—courage, good cheer—the sword I wield;
Sometimes a little stagger or slumber or stroll, but I hasten to that bold,
bright day by seeing the polished pearl;
A fury of the boisterous wind must not make me do a feeble back spin, but
a firm front swirl;
A fierce roar of the lion must not make me succumb flinchingly to its
superficial appeal;
A flimsy folding of the hands must not make me overlook repeatedly the
work ahead—yeah, a step further;
A copperhead serpent—at whim—flings its venomous seal;
Yet the warm glowing rainbow arc prods me a step further;
It's not over yet, but it's worth the blistering winter, the mild spring, the
scorching summer, and the chilly fall;
Not falling utterly in despair with a daring stare, but standing resiliently tall;
Once again, ready, resilient, resolved, resonant, revived, and wonderfully
reigning;

Beautiful benchmark words for reigning and regaining more plains;
From a too-long run-around;
A vital step further toward triumph in the final round;
And thereby declare it is worth the straining effort of stepping forward;
With sizzling heat, billowing smoke, and an onward press pushing toward;
A glorious mountain;
A perpetual fountain;
Round up the mound then;
The suffering and sweat from toil;
The pain and gain from toil;
The jubilee and joy that remains from toil;
A top-notch toil without taint;
A mind fervent, firm, and intact without faint;
Not emitting the shadowy smell of smoke perhaps makes me quaint;
For the furnace and the flame are the remaining brand of gain;
For the good of that one step further assures me that I'm not the same;

True Love

True love is not an ephemeral shadow,
Thus fleeting in the gleaming of the day,
Yet it stretches above and beyond any ominous trace of doubt—come what may.
It revives long-standing hope in every winnowed bellflower,
Thereby emitting redolence into the vernal zephyr…then pours gentle shower of the hour.
Though the routines of life are diurnal, 'tis love that, as a sweet fragrance,
projects a great light of hope inside life's journal,
For the depth of love's harmonious chord is more meaningful than the evanescence of a fickle feather,
Thereby shifting and vanishing into the boisterous winds of enraged, warlike weather.
Neither does it fade into the thick bosom of the whirling night,
Nor does it vacillate through the many sorrows of life's painful flights.
For it blooms from a bud;
It sparkles from soapsuds.
Its iridescence indeed can be seen,
After the gentle rain in the spring,
Displayed majestically in the sky before every human being,
For it dares every mortal with a sweet chuckle,
For it ever remains on the sacred pages of life as an ointment for mankind's bruised knuckle,
Oh! How I marvel at its sweet chord, conciliating and facilitating mankind from a chaotic world
Into a solid sparkling pearl,
Love is not apocryphal… 'tis tender, just, and undeniably genuine,

A secure, timeless passage, thereby gushing forth special drops of enthusiasm—send me one.
A splash on my stern face,
For it placates my presence, found in a pastoral land not to escape.

Parting the Way

Beyond the thick shroud of serenity in the southern vernal breeze, thus shifting dramatically into an even more soothing but less intense course,
With all of the inexorable shifts of change, I must now go my separate way,
For the progression of the Big Dipper suddenly appears vividly, as star after star hurls with a therapeutic crimson dome sky, thus featuring an anthem far more attractive than "The Star Spangled Banner."
A recrudescence with a brilliant appeal,
A grand slam ushering forth a magnificent symphony, thus harmonizing sweet melodies for life's celestial formations.
A ringing of cairnstones demonstrating that life is, in a sense, a phenomenal activity, which points toward "Parting the Way."
Bringing into being the gentle cry of an adorable babe snuggled with a tender, caring, and loving mom. Yet one day the babe will struggle perhaps as a wounded eaglet as it seeks "Parting the Way."
Reverberating deep into the Coral Sea, thus penetrating the deep, muddy land and, of course, its repercussions move across the frail surface waters as a clarion reminder that I must go my separate way…
You must go your separate way.
He or she must go his or her separate way… They must go their separate way. Life is a continuous cycle of changes.
I'm reminded that I must take time and pause from this rather brief philosophical discussion and once again go my separate way

as a full-grown eagle, here parting across the Grossglockner Mountains of Austria into the dazzling deep blue.

And yet, may the rugged path from which I adjourn be henceforth a surging reservoir of strength by which to share in our next hopeful assemblage.

Back Matter

Hear "The River" that ruffles across the shore into a whirlwind of storm. Then it lavishes simultaneously in all directions. In the calm of the day, this same river continues to drench the earth with its penetrable outpour—a thrust… a gush… a flush. Such a spectacular stream is able to pour throughout each of our minds, and as a reservoir, we are able to collect the springing waters as a special supply. So enjoy the stream as it seeks to plunge amazingly into our consciousness and also as it attempts to affect deeply our emotions.

www.ingramcontent.com/pod-product-compliance
Lightning Source LLC
Chambersburg PA
CBHW050014040726
47599CB00014B/1381

* 9 7 8 1 9 6 9 8 6 5 3 6 7 *